W9-BEF-047

stuff YOU already know*

*and everybody should

MAESTRO
PRESS

MAESTRO
PRESS

Maestro Press
8895 Towne Centre Dr. Suite 105-210
San Diego, CA 92122

www.MaestroPress.com
www.StuffYouAlreadyKnow.com

The anecdotes and advice herein are not intended to replace the services of trained mental health professionals. You are advised to consult with your health-care professional with regard to matters relating to your mental health, and in particular, regarding matters that may require diagnosis or medical attention. The author and publisher specifically disclaim any liability that is incurred from the use or application of the contents of this book.

The names and identifying characteristics of some of the individuals featured throughout this book have been changed to protect their privacy. Any resemblance to actual persons, living or dead, is purely coincidental.

Printed in the United States of America

First edition

No part of this publication may be reproduced, stored in or introduced into a retrieval system, or transmitted, in any form, or by any means (electronic, mechanical, photocopying, recording, or otherwise), without the prior permission of the publisher. Requests for permission should be directed to info@maestroconsultinggroup.com.

ISBN (US edition): 978-0-9896291-0-2

Library of Congress Cataloguing-in-Publication Data
DeLapa, Gina M.
Stuff you already know / Gina DeLapa.
1. Inspiration   2. Motivation   3. Conduct of life.

For Adam

Note to the Reader

If you've ever had something turn out so rewarding that you knew you couldn't take the credit, you'll know how I feel about having written this book.

It began with the simple desire to jot down some words of wisdom for my nephew Adam, who would soon be starting high school. I don't even remember how this idea popped into my head, although I'm sure it had something to do with H. Jackson Brown Jr.'s *Life's Little Instruction Book,* from the early 1990s.

What started as a journal filled with random, handwritten notes for my nephew eventually grew and took on a life of its own—one that I hope will touch *your* life, regardless of your age.

As you will see, some of these entries are silly, some are deep, and some are neither here nor there. It's probably best not to overthink them, or to read too much into their order.

Just as I did not set out to write a book, I did not set out to have three overarching themes—yet, here they are:

1. Set yourself up for success.

This is something my dad said to me in passing, when I was buying my first house. My dad, like a lot of dads, is funniest and most profound when he's not trying to be.

(The other profound thing my dad used to say to me was, *"Kick it in the ass!"* I would hear this every morning during my senior year of high school, when my dad insisted I drive his big-boat Lincoln to school in the crazy Vegas traffic—with him beside me. I hated the traffic, my foot barely reached the pedals, and the car had a bad habit of stalling whenever the light turned from red to green. As soon as it did, my father would yell, *"Kick it in the ass!"*)

Apart from this introduction, you won't find that sentiment anywhere in this book. But you'll find one similar at #273.

Entry #1 is simply, "Set yourself up for success." If you apply these words to any area of life, they will almost always shed light on what to do next, or how to do it better—from how to park (#183) to how to build a rewarding life (#23).

2. Take the high road.

Growing up, I don't remember hearing these words—but my mother taught them at every turn.

When I was about to turn five and didn't feel like inviting Patrick Cook to my birthday party, my mother asked me over breakfast in a matter-of-fact tone, "How do you think he would feel if you didn't include him?" Patrick came to the party, and as I recall, he stayed and helped clean up.

When I was eleven and wanted desperately to quit piano lessons, my mother didn't stop me—but she had *me* call my teacher. This is probably where I first learned #58.

In seventh grade, when I wanted to spend the night at Jenny Lange's house after I had already told Dawn Wilson I would go roller-skating, it was my mother who let me know, "It doesn't work that way." No, it doesn't. Hence, #200.

Finally, when I was still a brand-new driver, the orange padded roof of my mother's car met with an unfortunate scrape against a giant Dumpster (See #61). My mother groaned at the damages, put her arm around me in sympathy, and used a d-word I'd never heard before:

Deductible.

I spent that summer paying it off, through my job at the public library. And when I had paid back every penny, my mother told me how proud she was that I had risen to the challenge. I said, "Honey, you *made* me." She was proud anyway.

Taking the high road doesn't always feel warm and fuzzy. It can cost us our money, our time, and sometimes a piece of our hearts.

Yet it never costs us our souls. If anything, taking the high road *magnifies* our souls. It makes us better than we were. And what could be more—stop me before I use the word precious—but what could be more valuable than that?

3. Glorify God with your life.

You might be wondering why I'm including this, when most of the book deals with practical matters. But I think that's precisely where we show our love for God and neighbor: In our work habits. Our communication skills. Our hygiene. Everything. Spare me the holy man or woman who can't offer a decent apology, or the driver with a Jesus fish who hasn't learned to use a turn signal.

I suppose "Glorify God with your life" begins with an appreciation of your life—something I acquired gradually, starting as a young teenager. Childhood had been relatively easy. Yes, my parents worked us hard—harder than what I remember any of my friends going through—but that was mostly a good thing.

If my parents overlearned the lesson of industry, I overlearned the lesson of mortality, and this is where the story gets a little deep. When the first person in your world to die is a friend who just turned eleven, and you're not yet ten, it might not ruin your childhood, but it shifts your perspective in ways you're not even aware of.

Death was no longer the remote abstraction it should have been at age nine. It would take me years to figure out I would probably outlive my parents—and how cruel it is when this happens in reverse. (That's the problem, of course, with childhood losses: We have only a child's capacity to make sense of them.)

So when a second loss came at age twelve, equally sudden and senseless as the first, it was a little like being hit by a truck. My outlook on life grew considerably bleaker before it grew brighter.

What made the difference? My parents. God. The sacrament of Confession. A smart-alecky sense of humor (not in Confession), which brought me out of my shell and helped me to make friends in my new middle school. One of those friends is Gail, whose son Adam has known me his whole life as Aunt Gina and who first inspired this book.

If surviving adolescence isn't a source of unending gratitude, I don't know what is.

May you see my gratitude on every page. And however you define yourself spiritually or otherwise, I invite you to filter these thoughts through the lens of your own life, and to keep and pass along only what is helpful.

Gina DeLapa
San Diego, California
July 2013

P.S. Wherever you see a web link, that's your invitation to receive more goodies online.

P.P.S. Please forgive the occasional Rated PG swear words. Neither the book nor my life would be the same without them.

1. ◆

Set yourself up for success.

You're the only one who can make this happen, and ultimately the only one who can keep it from happening.

2. Beware the many faces of fear, including indecision, endless preparation, education, or information-gathering.

3. Don't go to jury duty without your iPad.

4. Spend the extra money to protect expensive gadgets.

5. Read *How to Find Your Mission in Life* by Richard Nelson Bolles.

stuffyoualreadyknow.com/5

6. Anytime you're doing laundry, throw in at least one pair of underwear. Unless, of course, you're washing dish towels.

7. **Pay attention to how you feel.**

Rarely can you read another person's mind or motives, but you *can* tell when something feels okay and when it doesn't. Follow your gut.

8. My brother Tony's advice: Get married in your own shoes.

9. Never give your wife a gift from the drugstore—or the airport.

10. Beware the relationship that's high maintenance, low reward. Friendships in particular should be *fun*—not perpetual work.

stuffyoualreadyknow.com/10

---

11. Let all your relationships find their own level.

   We make relationships more stressful when we either (a) do less than our part, or (b) do much more than our part. The key is to live in the sweet spot in between. When we do, the result is something more beautiful than anything we could have imagined or strived for.

12. Floss nightly until it becomes a habit. Putting on your favorite music makes it less of a chore.

13. If something is important (like flossing), don't put it off until just before bedtime. You'll be too tired.

14. Put a coaster underneath your drink.

15. Don't give sarcastic birthday cards. Humorous, yes. Insulting or depressing, no.

stuff YOU already know…

16. Never assume or ask a woman if she's pregnant.

17. Never ask someone, especially an elder, who they voted for.

18. Base your relationships on love, not on obligation.

19. Develop a sincere, confident handshake—one that works equally well for men and women.

20. Never ridicule someone's name. Names are sacred.

21. When you go to family reunions, sit with the folks you *don't* see all the time. It's so easy to do the opposite.

22. Spring for the 100% cotton sheets.

23. Spend most of your time developing your gifts: the skills and attributes you enjoy using and the ones that make the world a better place.

24. Don't confuse forgiveness with reconciliation.

We're called to forgive—we're not always called to restore the relationship. Sometimes we need to let the relationship go, so we *can* forgive.

25. Remember that you are not obligated to read books that come your way unbidden. Not even this one.

26. Never criticize someone's hometown.

27.

If you think you owe somebody an apology, you probably do.

Keep it simple, but clear the air.

28. Pass the salt and pepper together, even if someone says, "Pass the salt." That's not my rule—that's just how it's done. It's more thoughtful than making someone also ask for the dang pepper.

29. When you rest the knife on your plate, point the blade inward so it's facing you, not someone else at the table.

30. When you're the host, it's your job to pick the restaurant. Or if you prefer, you can give your guest(s) a couple of options.

31. When you're the host, plan to arrive at the restaurant *before* your guests, so you're there to greet them. It's a little awkward if they have to greet you.

stuff YOU already know…

32. **Send meaningful thank-you notes.**

stuffyoualreadyknow.com/32

33. Always send a thank-you note to the prospective employer after the interview. The key is to send it soon, while the hiring decision is still being made.

34. If you're the employer, notify the candidates who did *not* get hired.

If you've ever called to check the status of your application, only to have the phone answered by the person who was hired in your place, you know why this is important.

35.

Take the **stairs**, preferably two at a time.

stuffyoualreadyknow.com/35

36. Take a phone charger with you when you travel. If you get stuck at the airport, you'll be glad you have it.

37. Before choosing a connecting airport, decide how you would feel about getting stranded there overnight.

38. Live so others are glad they trusted you, invited you, invested in you, helped you, and hired you.

39. Take notes on your own life.

When I was twenty-eight, I bought a white leather journal so I could keep track of what life was teaching me. It turns out what life was teaching me was sort of cheesy and sad. Not sad as in melancholy, but just sad and comical in terms of what I thought back then was so important.

But out of all that cheesiness ("Enjoy real hot cocoa"), I found a few keepers:

- Cultivate a rich private life.

- Remember that not everybody with class has money, and not everybody with money has class.

- Invoice promptly.

Tracking what you've learned is life affirming. It allows you to celebrate victories and draw good out of misfortune. It gets you to laugh and lighten up. It helps you to see patterns, and when necessary, rise above them. It inspires hope.

Keep track of what life has taught you, and you could shave years or decades off your learning curve. You might also find it becomes a lifelong habit, one you can proudly share with the next generation—which of course is the whole premise of this book.

40. If you made the call, make it your job to call back if you get disconnected.

41. Keep in mind that all news today is biased.

42. Choose carefully the influences you let into your life. What you let in today will become normal tomorrow.

43. Buy full-fat sour cream.

44. Resist the temptation to fight via text or email.

The more emotionally charged the message, the more personal the form of communication should be. At the very least, don't put the other person's words in quotation marks, as in, *I didn't "make" you do anything.* It's only going to fan the flames.

45. In times of stress, start and end your day with something enjoyable and normalizing.

46. When you get home from school or work, give yourself at least 15 minutes to shift gears. Use this time to …

- Put away your stuff.

- Change clothes.

- Grab a bite to eat.

- Decompress.

- Do whatever else you need to do.

47. Don't let someone else's character diminish your own.

48. Do something special for your mom on her birthday.

49. Do right by your enemies—not to change them, but so they don't change you.

This does not mean trying to like, trust, or respect someone who is not likeable, trustworthy, or respectable. It just means holding your head high, and as much as possible, doing the kind and decent thing. You'll sleep better.

50. *Give* a damn. Let your words and actions show you care.

If you're caring and competent, you can do just about anything. As Billy Joel said, "I've reached the age where competence is a turn-on."

51. Respond to every invitation, even if it's to politely decline.

52.

Don't go to your boss with a problem until you've already thought of a **solution.**

stuff YOU already know…

53. When you're the boss, don't let your direct reports "delegate up." Help them, but don't take on their work.

54. Never fall in love with someone's potential. Look for someone with whom you're fundamentally compatible from Day One.

55. Don't let anyone fall in love with *your* potential. The right person will love you for you.

56. There's always something good you can say about another person. If not, and you have to say something, try, "He makes good soup."

57. Steer clear of reckless behavior. You could never be replaced.

58. When you have to fire someone, get it out in the first sentence.

59. Remember the Golden Rule, but live by the Platinum Rule.

The Golden Rule says, "Do unto others as you would have done to you." The Platinum Rule says, "Do unto others as they would have done to themselves."

60. Place the name tag on your right lapel, so that when you go to shake hands, your name will be *more* prominent, not less.

61. When you mess up, fess up.

62. Beware the man or woman who can't be confronted.

Typically, if you tell someone, "You're stepping on my toe," the person will instinctively apologize and move their foot. That is, they'll change their behavior so they're no longer hurting you—especially if you confront them gently.

But what happens when you tell someone they're stepping on your toe—not physically, but emotionally? In a good relationship, the person will again instinctively apologize and (emotionally speaking) move their foot.

In other cases, you might get a much different response. If you notice that every preference or concern is met with denial, excuses, blame, meltdowns, mind games, or *whatever,* you're dealing with someone who can't be confronted—even when they're hurting you.

So how do you change that? You don't.

Instead, you do what's known as "bless and release." You let go of your expectations that things will be different, and, if necessary, you withdraw some of your emotional investment—not out of punishment but out of self-preservation.

Save your heart and energy for those who (a) care about their effect on you and (b) *can show it*. You need and deserve that—but it's up to you to make it happen.

63. When parting ways with your employer, leave at your peak and leave on good terms. It's a lot easier to jump from one peak to another than to find new work when your morale is in the gutter.

64. Don't grocery shop when you're hungry.

65. Don't date when you're lonely.

66. Never diss someone else's family member, even if they just did.

67. Don't diss someone else's friend, even if they just did.

68.

Remind yourself each morning, "My goal today is to feel *great*."

It'll inspire you to put up with *less* hassle, not more.

69. Keep your hands on the wheel and your eyes on the road. As the bumper sticker says, "Honk if you love Jesus, text if you want to meet him."

70. Never rob someone of their moment—their hope, joy, dignity, enthusiasm. Don't let anyone rob you of yours.

71. Whenever you're feeling stuck or out of sorts, ask yourself what you need—in the third person.

A massage-therapist friend used to ask me rhetorically (in the middle of a massage), "What does *Gina* need?" At first it sounded sort of juvenile, like something Mister Rogers would ask. But I have since found this question to be the fastest way to break a bad mood.

For one thing, talking about ourselves in the third person is funny. (Think of Chris Farley's line in *Tommy Boy*: "Tommy no likey.") Maybe the question also reminds us to treat ourselves like a friend.

Try it. Ask yourself right out loud, "What does (your name) need?" You might be surprised at the clarity of your answers.

stuffyoualreadyknow.com/71

72. Switch over to mechanical pencils. If you need a recommendation, I like the blue Quicker Clickers from Pentel, in 0.7 mm lead.

73. Make your bed in the morning. Small disciplines lead to larger ones.

74. Pick up your dirty clothes, even if you live alone.

75. When you want to splurge, splurge. Don't settle for frozen yogurt and turkey hot dogs.

76. Keep in touch with friends from childhood. The same things that crack you up at age thirteen will crack you up well into midlife.

77. No matter how bad things get, keep the faith and press on. Your being here matters. In the words of Wayne Dyer, "You make all of humanity complete."

78. If you feel you can't go on, stop reading and call the National Suicide Prevention Lifeline. In the U.S., their number is 1-800-273-8255.

79. Don't dismiss wise words just because you don't like the source.

stuff YOU already know…

80.

As long as you live, stay **open and** teachable—not passive or gullible, but always eager to **learn** new things.

81.   Never be in a hotel room late at night without at least a Snickers bar and a bottle of water.

82.   When you leave a tip for the housekeeping staff, leave it on the desk or dresser, not on the nightstand. It sends a better message.

83.   Walk fast. It's impossible to pout and power walk at the same time.

84.   When someone says, "You look like you're on a mission!" as they will when you walk fast, smile and say, *"Always."*

85.   If you have to walk past someone else, especially an elder or anyone else with mobility issues, do so *gently*.

86. Don't let anyone make you feel less-than.

87. Know which hills are worth dying on, and which ones aren't.

88. Vent to let it go, not to drive the wound deeper.

89. Don't mangle the stick of butter.

90. Preserve family recipes.

91. Wear cologne sparingly, if at all. Instead of spraying it on directly, spray it into the air, then walk through it.

92. Remember that everyone is carrying a heavy load.

Two people dear to me have just lost a mother and a father, and what occurs to me is how neither one is the type to wear their sorrow on their sleeve. Which means if you didn't know them, you would never know their worlds have just been radically altered, and that underneath their smiles they are missing someone terribly.

What's true for them is true for us, and true for every person we meet. Each of us is carrying something—a sorrow, a guilt, an irreplaceable loss—something. We might not know what that something is, and we don't have to.

The point is, if we keep in mind that everyone is carrying a heavy load—from the co-worker next to us to the guy on the freeway—we'll not only be kinder than necessary, we'll find it impossible to be anything less.

93.

Make sure the people you love and appreciate *know* they are loved and appreciated.

94. To keep the wine bottle from dribbling, twist it as you're pouring.

95. When a couple you know has a baby, consider getting a gift for the *parents*.

96. Keep snacks in your car so you don't starve. One of my favorites: mixed nuts from The Peanut Roaster (peanut.com).

97. Never walk in to apply for a job unless you're well dressed, well groomed, and carrying a decent pen.

stuffyoualreadyknow.com/97

98. If you don't like someone, don't go camping with them.

stuff YOU already know...

99. Count your blessings. The more you count, the more you will find.

100. To become a better writer, read excellent writing.

101. Steer clear of anyone doing drugs.

The moment someone starts, that's your cue to leave. It isn't about passing judgment—it's about you not getting in trouble with the law. And not tempting fate. You can't do drugs if you're not in the room with them.

102. Always wipe the hair out of the sink and tub, especially when staying at someone else's home, but also in your own home.

103. If your enthusiasm is making others uncomfortable, scale back.

104.

Resist the
temptation
to tell stories
that aren't
yours to tell.

stuff YOU already know…

105. Never confuse a good college with the one that's best for you.

I had just told my friend Bobby, who lived in my dorm, I was transferring to Michigan State.

"Do you really think it's a better school?"

He sounded stunned. Northwestern was the better school. But it was also like a fine pair of shoes that pinched my feet, mercilessly.

For one thing, there was nothing at Northwestern I wanted to major in. Journalism had turned out to be too newspaper focused, and from my nineteen-year-old point of view, English majors wrote for other English majors. So ten days after leaving Northwestern, I began my junior year at Michigan State, and less than two years later graduated with a degree in advertising. Best decisions ever. But that's another story for another day.

I have since learned some things about choosing a university, especially after having worked for two of them and having interacted with countless students:

- Look for socioeconomic diversity, not just geographic diversity. As one student put it, college should *prepare* you for the real world—not shelter you from it.

- Choose a school in a true college town, not in a town that wishes you and all your friends weren't there. At the very least, make sure you understand and are okay with the school's relationship to the wider community.

- Go where you will fit in and grow, not where you'll be struggling constantly to keep up.

The older I get, the happier I am that I transferred to Michigan State—and the more thankful I am for the two years at Northwestern. Who wouldn't want to live near Chicago, or go to school on a campus that overlooked Lake Michigan?

More poignantly, Northwestern helped me become a better writer—not just for English majors, but for the far-more-fascinating multitude.

106.

Use your public library.

107. In food and school and work and life, presentation counts.

108. Don't let anyone talk to you over the top of their glasses—it's rude.

109. As much as possible, keep your sense of humor.

For example, if you're ever asked by a multilevel marketing recruiter, "Are you as happy as you *could* be?" answer with a cheerful and emphatic *Yes.* They have nowhere to go with that.

110. Anytime you're talking to the media, ask to respond to their questions via email. This will reduce your risk of being misquoted or quoted out of context.

111. Before you vote by absentee ballot, make sure your vote will be counted *before* the election results, not after.

112. Turn on a light before entering a dark room. There's nothing fun about tripping or stubbing your toe.

113. Once or twice a year, take yourself to Denny's.

114. Pay attention. If a man cheats at golf, he'll cheat in business.

> *Friendly disclaimer:* I don't play golf. But I have heard this sentiment from enough golfers I know and trust to believe it to be true.

115. Choose your fundraisers carefully. There's something off about an all-you-can-eat breakfast to support the (starving) people of Haiti.

116. If you don't recognize the name or number, don't answer the phone.

117. Never ever use the R-word, and politely stop those who do. For more information, visit r-word.org.

118. Remember that every person has something to teach you.

119. Remember that every *job* has something to teach you.

Here are five things I learned from my mercifully brief stint at Billy's Roasted Chicken Palace:

- If you don't have a twist tie, you can still close a garbage bag by twirling the top around your index fingers and tying the two ends together.

- Everyone should have at least one job in their life where they're required to wear a hairnet—and a brown polyester uniform.

- There's no shame in cleaning public toilets—but I can't say that I miss it.

- There are plenty of after-school jobs that won't leave you smelling like bleach and french fries. Billy's wasn't one of them.

- Misunderstanding comes with the territory, as in my Uncle Dave's question, "Does Gina have to dress like a chicken?"

120. When interviewing for a job, pay attention to how you get along with your prospective boss.

Much of your on-the-job happiness or misery will be driven by this relationship. I say this with all due respect to *my* former bosses, most or all of whom I'm still in touch with. Well, not the one from Billy's. You can't win 'em all, nor should you try.

121. Never think you have to earn God's love.

122. Go out of your way to be cheerfully low maintenance.

123. Listen to Jim Rohn's audio program, *The Art of Exceptional Living*. I've been listening to it since 1993, and I still get good things out of it.

stuffyoualreadyknow.com/123

124. Use a yellow highlighter. It's easy to read through and won't show up when you copy the page.

125.

Respect the difference between **secrecy** and **privacy**.

Secrecy implies withholding information that someone else has a right to know, because it is timely and pertinent to the relationship. As in, "Mom, I just put a big scrape in your car."

Privacy is about *your* business, or you and your spouse's business. You can share your private world with whomever you wish—but you're not obligated to share it with everyone who asks.

126. When making group decisions, always add your two cents. Saying "I don't care" only keeps things stuck.

127. Get investment advice from your stockbroker and tax advice from your CPA. Don't try to mix the two.

128. Hire the best advisors you can, and do your best to follow their recommendations.

129. Develop good listening skills. In the words of Martin Luther King Jr., "Riot is the language of the unheard."

130. Beware the job that looks good and sounds good, but leaves you unfulfilled.

stuff YOU already know…

131. Pay attention to how people behave when no one else is around. Who we are in private is who we really are.

132. Make a point of not complaining, criticizing, or correcting others when it really isn't necessary.

133. Write "See Photo ID" on the signature block of your credit cards. It can't hurt and it might help.

134. When handing over a credit card that says "See Photo ID" on the back, offer your ID at the same time.

135. Don't try to tame a scorpion.

Some people, for whatever reason, aren't capable of loving us and may even enjoy hurting us.

136.

Take time for silence, just to air out your brain, hear yourself think, and let in a wisdom beyond your own.

137. Recognize when taste trumps nutrition. If you've ever tried no-salt cottage cheese, you know what I'm talking about.

138. Beware of dealing with people who have the power to say no, but don't have the power to say yes.

139. Stick with brands you know and like—you'll save money and simplify your life.

140. If you walk out the door feeling as though you're forgetting something, you probably are. Take a moment to figure out what it is.

141. Steer clear of meetings without an agenda.

stuffyoualreadyknow.com/141

142. Stick to your allotted time when giving a speech.

> Better yet, end a touch early. No speaker ever lost points with the audience for ending early.

143. My brother John's advice: Don't go to a wedding reception on an empty stomach.

144. Leave voice mails that are short and to the point. Include your phone number, stated slowly, at the beginning and end of your message.

145. Even in your closest relationships, allow for a little mystery—and breathing room.

> As Aunt Donna used to say, "I need to go away so you can miss me." And as my friend Jen's mother likes to say, "Let's not be like butt and underwear."

146. Never deliver terrible news via voice mail, especially if it's unexpected. Ask instead for the person to call you.

147. People grieve in different ways, sometimes in odd or messy ways. As much as you can, let them.

148. Never show up to the party early.

149. Let your whole life exude kindness and class.

150. Draw a line in the sand.

Most toxic situations won't go away until you declare yourself done. Occasionally this requires saying something to another person— oftentimes it does not.

151. When you're having trouble with a website, try viewing it in another browser.

152. Whenever you're faced with a dilemma, remember that however you handle it this time will be that much easier to repeat next time.

153. When going to a meeting, bring your own water.

154. When emailing a group of people who don't know each other, protect their privacy by using the blind-copy option.

155. Raise your kids with the Tim Russert philosophy: "You are always, always loved, but you are never, never entitled."

156.

Skip the backstory.
If you're running
late, just say you're
running late
and when you'll
be there.

---

157. Treat everyone with respect, even when you're not feeling it. That's how you maintain self-respect.

158. Unless it serves a noble purpose, please don't be a martyr.

Martyrs give more than they can reasonably give—even when no one else has asked them to. They take care of others at the expense of taking care of themselves, even when it's unnecessary.

I'm always afraid that people in this category are going to snap—like Ned Flanders in the *Simpsons* episode, "Hurricane Neddy."

If you find yourself becoming resentful or otherwise hard to live with, it's probably time to start tending to your own needs. This is not an act of selfishness, it's an act of courage and wisdom—one that will benefit everyone you care about, including yourself.

159. Don't take medical advice from Dr. Google.

160. Steer clear of tanning beds.

161. Don't leave the party without saying goodbye to the host.

162. When something falls off the calendar, do not schedule something else in its place.

163. Resist the temptation to tell someone how tall they are, how short they are, how they look just like Norm on *Cheers,* etc. They've heard it.

164.

Keep your eye on the prize.

Don't let yourself get delayed or distracted.

165. Get good at making time work for you.

stuffyoualreadyknow.com/165

166. Join Toastmasters, preferably early in your career. The confidence and public-speaking skills you'll gain will serve you the rest of your life.

167. Don't try to win everyone's approval.

You're going to meet people who go through life blaming the mirror for what it reflects. Sometimes that mirror will be you. Don't back down, don't rub it in, and don't take it personally.

To put it more bluntly, some folks are going to reject you not for your faults, but for your virtues. For example, when you're professional, conscientious, happy, or kind,

you're going to meet with resistance—
sometimes fierce resistance—from those who
aren't. Your good qualities remind them of what
they could and should be but are not.

It's not your fault, and it's not your thing to fix.
Smile, detach, and move forward, taking all
your virtues with you.

168. Before you pick up your date, clean out
your car.

169. If you want to lose weight, make weightlifting
a core part of your exercise routine. *Reason:*
Muscle burns fat, and muscle raises
metabolism.

170. Learn proper weight-lifting technique—that's
how you avoid injury and Popeye arms.

171.

Don't expect your employer to take care of you.

That's your job, not theirs.

172. Limit your exposure to those who are constantly disapproving, even mildly so.

173. If you're bored or otherwise out of sorts, grab a garbage bag and pick up the trash on your block. You'll feel better.

174. Focus on solutions, not on rehashing problems. Keep asking, "Where do we go from here?"

175. If you're sick, stay home.

176. Save the details of your illness for your nurse.

Remember as a kid how scared you felt when you had to tell your mom you were too sick to go to school?

If your experience was anything like mine, you

stood outside your parents' closed bedroom door, fidgeting with your pajamas and nervously preparing your case before finally knocking—feebly, of course.

And even if your mother accepted your stammering speech and let you stay home, there was always that one sibling who taunted, *"You're not sick!"* The worst was when they were right.

Here's my theory: For many of us, those experiences seep into adulthood. We don't want our boss, clients, or co-workers to think we're faking, so we go out of our way to paint our illness in graphic detail. We think we're building the relationship, when in reality we're just grossing someone out. It's happened to me more times than I can count.

Next time you have to call in sick, try simply saying, "I'm not feeling well, and I'm not going to make it in today." That's all most people want or need to know.

177. When someone is holding back information you need to know, and you've tried everything else, try asking politely, "What is it you're not telling me?"

178. Hold private phone conversations in private, not in the grocery store.

179. If you don't already own it, get the Creedence Clearwater Revival album, *Willy and the Poor Boys*. It never gets old.

stuffyoualreadyknow.com/179

180. Remember that the better the band, the less likely it is you'll find their best material on their Greatest Hits.

stuff YOU already know…

181. Never ever refer to someone as an "accident."

Every human life, planned or unplanned, is sacred.

182. Trust your friend's directions more than your GPS.

183. Park your car in a getaway position.

It's easier to pull away than to have to back up or turn around, especially in the dark.

184. Err on the side of generosity.

185.

Don't make life harder than it is.

stuff YOU already know...

186. Don't make death harder than it is.

Susie was my friend from age four up. Like a lot of childhood best friends, we confided our hearts and laughed ourselves senseless—the best times were when we did both.

One Sunday when we were in high school, the two of us were driving around in her mother's crème de menthe-colored Cadillac. I told Sue how nervous I was about starting driver's ed the next day.

Immediately she whipped into the empty parking lot of Hilltop Foods, stopped the car, and said, "Switch seats with me. You're driving." I did—white-knuckled and laughing as the car jerked us along at about seven miles per hour. (Kids, do not try this at home.)

Fast-forward to a cold, snowy morning in January 2009. I'm standing before a classroom full of ninth graders I've never met, giving an interactive talk titled "Leading a Life of Eternal Significance." The atmosphere is polite, but not

---

…and *everybody* should

very interactive—and eternally significant only in the sense that time is crawling.

So I take a deep breath and tell the class, "Raise your hand if you've got a best friend." Forty hands shoot up. "On the count of three, I want you to shout out the name of your best friend. One. Two. Three."

Damon! Jackie! Eduardo! Maria! Immediately, the whole room is animated—except for me. I take another breath, wondering how I'm going to get through this.

"Let me tell you about *my* childhood best friend," I begin. "Susie." I tell the class how smart she was, how many friends she had, how I could never keep up with her. About all the fun we had, starting in preschool.

About the first time I saw her drunk at the beginning of ninth grade—not at a loud party but on a quiet Sunday afternoon. About the bewilderingly bad decisions she made that drove our worlds further and further apart, how in our adult years she ended every phone call by telling me how much she loved me—and of course I told her how much I loved her, too. How after hearing her blithely describe her latest troubles, I hung up the phone and thought, *"My goodness. I hope the next time I see her, I don't start crying."*

"The next time I saw her," I continued, "I did not start crying. But the next time I saw her, she was in a box about this big. In the back of Saint Basil Catholic Church, four days after Christmas, and about one minute before the start of her memorial Mass. Accidental overdose."

By now, the kids are staring at me, bug-eyed. "Look around this room," I told them, "and stick with the friends who bring out your best, not your worst—and *be* that kind of friend."

Miraculously, we managed to move on to lighter topics. At one point, the teacher smiled and signaled from the back of the room. "Ten more minutes," she said.

No sooner had I opened up the floor for questions when a small boy on the inside aisle shot up his hand. I gestured, inviting him to speak.

"Do you think there's anything more you could have done to save your friend?"

Shattered.

I stared down at him in disbelief. *Could a kid really be that cruel?* His big blue eyes locked onto mine, and suddenly I realized he wasn't being cruel—he was searching for answers. And I had better give him a real one.

"I've thought about that a lot," I sighed. Probably every day for the last two years. This was the first time I had ever said so out loud, or even to myself.

"Susie had all kinds of support," I told the class. "But she also had addictions. And if the love of a father, a brother, a sister, or a good friend could have saved her, I think she would have been saved, long ago."

---

stuff YOU already know…

The kid who asked the question nodded intently.

"We can do the part that is ours," I continued—as much for my sake as the students'. "But sometimes the extended hand is not grasped. And when things don't go as we had planned, we can and should let ourselves grieve. But we need not go *looking* for grief, or guilt. They'll find *us.*"

"In the meantime, we can live, we can laugh, and we can hope. We must."

Susan's memorial Mass opened with the familiar hymn, "Be Not Afraid." Afterward, I went home and carefully wrote one line on my quote board: *"You shall see the face of God and live."*

These are the words that sustain my hope, and comfort my heart—even through the questions that still pierce it now and then.

187. Allow yourself to experience joy, even when happiness is impossible.

The morning of my friend Susan's memorial Mass, I left for the church at the last possible minute, because I couldn't bear to say goodbye. Finally, I dragged myself to the car, climbed in, buckled up, and began the journey: sixty-six miles of sober, dry-eyed, unforgettable silence.

Despite the occasion, being at church that day brought an odd sense of joy—standing with Sue's family, standing next to my mother, knowing we were exactly where we needed to be, even if our hearts were on the ground.

This same paradox holds true in your life. Think of the times you've had to set aside your own comfort to come through for someone else, and the experience left you feeling anything but happy.

But you came through anyway. You did the good you were called to do—maybe not perfectly, but with a noble spirit that somehow proved to be enough. Let that be a comfort that nothing and no one can take from you.

188. Ask for help when you need it—including God's help, including professional help. One is no substitute for the other.

189. Never ask a woman if she colored her hair.

190. Don't reinforce bad behavior. What gets rewarded gets repeated.

191. Start the week on a full tank of gas.

192. If you're checking your luggage, pack as though you'll never see your stuff again. You might not.

193. Listen to the voice message *before* returning the call.

194. Let your language show you're a person of intelligence, character, and the 21ˢᵗ century.

195. Color outside the lines, but park between them.

196. Don't throw gum on the ground. Those who rely on wheelchairs will thank you for not messing up their (expensive) mode of transportation.

197. My brother Jim's advice: Don't be afraid to make some mistakes.

I would add, "Don't be afraid to *admit* your mistakes." That's how you grow. That's how you turn setbacks into rocket fuel.

stuffyoualreadyknow.com/197

198. Grate your own Parmesan.

199. When traveling outside the country, make sure your emergency contact has a passport, too. If anything happens to you, you'll want that person with you pronto—not six weeks from now.

200. Don't cancel plans with someone just because you get a better offer. It's disrespectful.

201. When the customer is ready to buy, let him. Many a sale has been lost because the salesperson kept talking.

202. Breathe.

203. Take a personal day on your birthday.

204.

Be a problem-solver.

No matter how tough the job market, there will always be a demand for those who can show they know how to solve problems.

stuff YOU already know…

205. Give yourself one day a week to wake up without an alarm.

206. Add the attachment *before* you write the email.

207. If an email is crucial or sensitive, wait till you're done writing and editing before filling in the recipient's name.

208. Show appreciation for your boss—he or she needs acknowledgment, just like you do.

209. Cut your parents some slack. They, too, had imperfect parents, as did we all.

210. Have friends of all ages.

211. If you truly wish to understand someone, get to know their pet peeves.

I guess I just assumed everybody liked the song "Brandy (You're a Fine Girl)." To me, it's one of those classics that my generation missed out on. Given the choice, I'll take Looking Glass over Madonna or Dexys Midnight Runners any day.

But I have baby-boomer girlfriends who *hate* "Brandy." Just hate it. To the point where they get angry if you bring it up (which never fails to *crack* me up). And not just because the song's about a man who prefers a body of water to the body and soul of a woman—or because Brandy still loves him, even after that ship has sailed.

No. My baby-boomer friends hate the song for all the things it reminds them of: Awkward dances in the darkened high-school cafeteria. Teenage boys with Coke-bottle glasses, long hair, and thready mustaches—and steamy breath, the kind you get from eating

Milk Duds. Throw in adolescent laughter, à la Beavis and Butt-Head, and it's no wonder "Brandy (You're a Fine Girl)" sends some people right over the edge.

Pet peeves are, by definition, negative and personal. Some are funny, some are serious. All of them teach us something about who we are and what we value.

212. Unless they're interfering with your mental health, honor your pet peeves—and those of others.

213. Steer clear of bombastic TV and radio shows.

214. Unless there's an immediate danger, don't yell at anyone.

215. Don't let anyone yell at you. It's uncivilized.

> You are not obligated to stay in a conversation with anyone who is shouting or otherwise being abusive. To do so does both of you a disservice—as does retaliating. Don't let yourself get sucked into the other person's rage or drama.

216. Know when to repair and when to replace.

217. Let backhanded compliments roll off your back. They're not about you.

218. Plan Sunday dinner so you'll have leftovers for Monday.

219. Knock before entering a public restroom stall.

220. Fly during the middle of the week—Tuesday, Wednesday, or Thursday—when airport traffic is lightest.

221. Question your assumptions.

I offer this in memory of my Grandma DeLapa, who went to go see *The Godfather*, thinking it was a religious movie.

222. Don't ascribe motives.

223. Be crystal clear about your own motives, and clean up the selfish ones.

224. Drink plenty of water before and after giving blood.

stuffyoualreadyknow.com/224

225. Keep a Sharpie fine-point marker in your kitchen.

226. Aim to read two books per month.

stuffyoualreadyknow.com/226

227. If you want to sleep well at night, turn off the news at least ninety minutes before bedtime.

228. Don't imagine that anyone's life is easy. It isn't.

229. Please don't serve potato salad with homemade Italian meatballs.

One night while visiting with my friends Vincent and Kathy, Vincent asked if sometime in the near future I would make my Aunt Anne's famous meatballs.

Subliminal message: They're a lot of work.
(They're also sort of sacred. I think every family has a recipe like that.) So when Kathy plopped down a big bowl of potato salad next to the meatballs I had just made, I think I said something.

We had a good laugh about it, but the point is, meatballs and potato salad *really don't go together.* It would be like you inviting me over for your signature spareribs, and me plunking down a can of Cheez Whiz.

Anytime you're throwing a dinner party, no matter how informal, you're better off taking charge of the menu. And you're well within your rights to do so.

stuffyoualreadyknow.com/229

230. Share recipes.

231.

Question the world around you.

As my old co-worker Tim used to say, "Who decided to make toilet paper that size?"

stuff YOU already know…

232. Get the bendy straws—they're more functional and more fun.

233. At least once in your life, live near a Trader Joe's.

234. Refuse to think of yourself as a victim.

Horrible things happen. When they happen to us, there's no pretending everything is fine.

Victimhood occurs when our hurts become something we cling to, and then a way of relating to the world, and finally a weapon by which we justify hurting others.

Most of us have fallen into the victim trap. I know I have. Once when I was complaining to a priest friend for the hundredth time about the same injustice, he smiled and said, "You're drinking the poison and expecting the other guy to die."

235. Don't encourage other people's victimhood.

236. Take a daily multivitamin.

237. Let your generosity be fueled by gratitude, not guilt.

238. Go for respect, not for being liked. In the words of Dr. Bernie Siegel, "If you need to be liked, you're in trouble."

239. Accept there will be times when you're not understood or are misunderstood.

240. Never miss an opportunity to speak a kind word or to do a kind deed. Most people aren't suffering from too much appreciation.

241. When a co-worker is grieving, maybe you can't say the right thing. But you can listen, and you can offer some way to lighten their workload.

242. Before helping a person with a disability, ask permission.

243. Give radically but not recklessly.

I once went to hear a talk by a local champion for the homeless. During the Q&A, somebody asked if we should give money to people on the street.

"Never, never, never," he said. *Reason:* It's tax-free income, with no strings attached. He recommended offering a card instead with the address of his shelter, which offers not only a meal and a bed but a much-needed sense of community and accountability.

I have given to the person on the street, and

I have politely withheld giving to the person on the street. I think the point for each of us is to act out of compassion and the best interests of the one who asks—irrespective of how we do it or how it looks to other people.

244. Tour a local homeless shelter, and find out how you can be part of the solution.

Unlike some of my friends and former students, I have never been homeless. But if you have ever toured a homeless shelter, you know it can forever alter how you look at folks on the street.

A month or two after taking a tour, I attended the graduation ceremony for those who had just completed the shelter's twelve-month recovery program.

Boy, it's so true what they say: Nobody knows how to party like people in recovery. There was more raucous joy in that church than I've felt at most Michigan State games.

You know it's going to be an emotional ceremony when you're wiping away tears and the whole thing hasn't even started: in my case, tears of exuberance for the ones who made it, tears of regret for one who did not. But tonight was pure celebration.

The twenty-five men and women who walked down the aisle to receive their diplomas could have been your co-workers. Their faces exuded such a quiet dignity, you might have wondered, as I did, how in the world they got there.

During the ceremony, three of the graduates stood up to speak. Though there's not room here to recount their stories, suffice it to say these were ordinary people who, through no fault of their own, had been hit with the unthinkable. How do you pull yourself up by the bootstraps when you lose your mother at age ten, or when you grow up seeing your father routinely beating your mother?

Yet despite everything these graduates had

been through (yes, including their own admittedly poor choices), their stories ended in triumph. Over and over again, they credited God—not as an afterthought but as the first words out of their mouths—for helping them overcome addictions, reunite their families, and contribute to the world through honest work.

One man who had stumbled into the shelter with black eyes and cracked ribs now stood before us in a suit and tie, proudly describing the corporate job he had started four weeks earlier, and how that very day he had deposited his first two-week paycheck.

"Miracles do happen," he said. "You're lookin' at one."

These are the reasons I support this shelter: to celebrate those who made it, to honor the ones who never made it to the front door, and to know the privilege of taking part in miracles. Care to join me?

stuffyoualreadyknow.com/244

245.

Sit near the front of the classroom.

You'll be less distracted and more alert.

246. Sit near the front at church—you'll be less distracted by the folks who walk in late.

247. I know it isn't manly to take a bath, but after a hard workout, it really does help to soak in a bath of Epsom salt.

248. Be a little cautious in your assertions.

For example, instead of saying, "You didn't attach the file," say, "I didn't see the file. Would you please resend it?"

249. Never brag about how you slacked off in school. People who do this reveal much about their character and judgment.

stuff YOU already know…

250.

Don't botch your own credibility.

For example, don't start a meeting with "I have a cold," a presentation with, "I'm just going to wing it," or a speech with, "I'm not much of a speaker."

251. Use CharityNavigator.org to make wise giving decisions. It's free.

Then *contribute* to Charity Navigator. Only one half of one percent of visitors do.

stuffyoualreadyknow.com/251

252. Protect your time.

253. Don't play devil's advocate.

254. Be patient and kind to the end, but recognize there may have to be an end.

255. Don't waffle, especially on matters of ethics or morality.

stuff YOU already know…

256. Do the right thing, even when it's horribly awkward—that's how minor miracles happen.

I had just parked my dusty red rental car and cracked open the door, when a gust of wind flung the door wide open—smacking it into the unoccupied car next to me. *Bam!*

Naturally, the other car looked showroom new. But now its white passenger-side door handle had a red-and-black divot the size of my thumb.

I thought of that urban legend about the guy who sideswipes a parked car and stops to assess the damage. Seeing others watching, he leaves the following note for the owner: "By accident I sideswiped your car and tore off your mirror. The people who are watching think I'm leaving you my name and number. I'm not."

I left my name and number. And after placing the carefully written sticky note underneath the owner's driver-side wiper, I was all too happy to get back in my car and scoot out of there.

Driving away, I sent up a prayer for the driver—and maybe for a little rain. Kidding. But if you've ever gone out of your way to do the decent thing, only to have it blow up in your face, you'll understand my ambivalence.

Sure enough, the next morning, right before catching my first flight home, my phone rang. It was the owner of the white car. I pictured having to hold the phone at arm's length while she screamed at me. Instead, she thanked me. We chatted for a few moments. It turns out the car *was* new. She said she and her husband knew the owner of a repair shop, and we agreed she would send me the bill so I could take care of it.

Grand total: less than fifty dollars. By the end of the week, the repair-shop owner had his payment, the car would be restored, and that was that. Or so I thought.

A few hours after hanging up with the repair-shop guy, the following text came in from the car owner:

"I am a believer that everything happens for a reason. You came along right at a time when I was questioning goodness in people and restored my faith. God bless."

And then she added a smiley face.

To share the exchanges that followed, or the uncanny circumstances surrounding them, would cheapen the whole encounter. But in a minor mishap that no one would have chosen, the private prayers of two complete strangers were answered in each other.

257. Follow up and follow through. If you do this consistently, you will stand out from the crowd, in the best sense of the word.

258. If you're trying to console somebody, don't start a sentence with, "At least." It doesn't help. Likewise for, "I know just how you feel."

259.

When someone you know is hurting, do much more listening than talking.

stuff YOU already know…

260. Anytime you cancel out on someone, make it *your* job to get the plans back on track.

Rather than putting the ball in the other person's court, offer some dates and times when the two of you could reschedule. Make it as easy as possible—not on yourself, but on the other person. That's how you show respect and build the relationship.

261. When you're the only one at the party not drinking the Kool-Aid, it's time to find a new party.

262. When the time is right, go to grad school. Just make sure you have a reasonably clear plan for what you want to get out of it.

stuffyoualreadyknow.com/262

263. Unless your doctor says you need them, don't bother with expensive shoe inserts.

264. Think twice before buying shoes that don't bend—or that bend in the middle, instead of where your foot does.

265. Surround yourself with service providers you like, trust, and respect—and who are easy to work with. You're paying these folks to be in your life.

266. Don't say, "No problem" in response to something that was never understood to be a problem.

267. Pace yourself.

stuff YOU already know…

268. Tip fairly. Even with a free-breakfast voucher, the server still deserves a tip on the full value.

269. Smile at the speaker and make eye contact, even if it's a big audience. The speaker will notice and appreciate it.

270. Remember that no one outside a marriage knows what goes on inside it.

271. Watch the documentary *The Rocky Saga: Going the Distance* and try telling me you can't get more done.

272. Make plans for your life, under God, or else be prepared to settle for someone else's plans.

273.

Kick yourself harder in the ass than anyone else.

Self-discipline is always easier and more rewarding than discipline imposed by a boss, a spouse, a parent, or anyone else.

274. Celebrate the longer days by using Siri to track the sunset.

275. Compliment people on things that matter to them. A compliment on something trivial can come across as an insult.

276. Don't borrow trouble. Remember the *Saturday Night Live* parody of a brand of jeans called "Bad Idea."

277. When high performance matters, hire a good trainer or coach.

Choose someone who can help you reach your destination faster, accomplish more than you could on your own, and who will make the journey more rewarding, not less.

And look for professionals who are passionate about what you're hiring them for—not those whose true passions lie elsewhere.

278. When entering or exiting a parking garage, turn your headlights on and your stereo off.

279. Call it for what it is. If it's cheating, call it cheating. If it's a bus, don't call it a motor coach.

280. Every few years, reread George Orwell's essay, "Politics and the English Language."

stuffyoualreadyknow.com/280

281. Keep track of the books you read each year.

Your list will help you retain what you've read, pass along good books to others, and see patterns in your life you didn't see before.

282. Don't go to bed hungry.

283. Don't go to bed with an untreated headache.

284. Be fair to those you do business with. Even when you're the customer, don't ask for more than your share.

285. Don't internalize other people's drama. Just let *them* own it.

286. Listen to others, but decide for yourself.

287. Notice how the people who remain friends aren't necessarily the ones with the most in common—they're the ones who place a similar value on the friendship.

288. If you're a kid and anyone ever says, "Don't tell your mom or dad," make sure that's the first thing you do.

289. Don't let anyone speak ill of your parents.

290. When talking to kids, get down on their level so you're eyeball to eyeball.

291. Ask permission before petting someone else's dog.

292. Ignore gossip.

293. Label behavior, but not people.

294. Don't listen to anyone who tries to label you.

stuff YOU already know...

295. When hiring a caterer or any other professional, look for someone who is two steps ahead of you, not one step behind.

296. Say OR-uh-gun, not OR-uh-gahn.

297. Say New OR-linz, not New or-LEENZ.

298. When something really matters to you, don't ask permission. Ask, "What would it take … ?"

299. My brother John's advice (not to me): "Lead, don't dominate."

300. Lead, don't "facilitate." The world needs more leaders, not more facilitators.

301.

Learn to distinguish between **honesty** and **integrity**. Integrity includes honesty, but goes beyond it.

stuffyoualreadyknow.com/301

302. Keep self-esteem in perspective.

There was no trace of weirdness when my college roommate Ginna gave me Nathaniel Branden's book *The Six Pillars of Self-Esteem* for my thirtieth birthday. For one thing, Ginna's a good friend—and we both had decent self-esteem to begin with.

Inside the cover, she wrote, "I hope you enjoy this as much as I did!" Even now, I love how the inscription embodies the very quality that self-esteem needs for its completion: namely, humility. My friend wasn't saying, "You need this, and I don't."

Without humility, self-esteem hardens into mere narcissism. But without self-esteem, we turn into doormats, which is obviously no good either.

Here are just some of the things healthy self-esteem makes possible—personally, professionally, and organizationally:

- Taking risks.

- Bouncing back from defeat.

- Enjoying our successes and the successes of others (maybe not our competitors').

- Addressing bad behavior without tearing down the person.

- Forgiving and moving on, after an offense or perceived offense.

- Owning up to mistakes, and when it's called for, saying, "I'm sorry."

- Paying a compliment.

- Showing the highest respect for others, while including ourselves in the equation.

- Giving freely, without undue expectations.

- Reading the writing on the wall.

- Changing before we have to.

These abilities are available to any of us, regardless of age, education, income, or career status. I know a ten-year-old who does most or all of the things on this list. What about us?

303. Keep investing in yourself and others. Your contributions will increase in ways you can't yet imagine.

304. If you're the boss, don't be the buddy.

305. Beware of a lot of unrecognizable initials after someone's name.

306. Unless you're getting paid for it, don't be anyone's therapist.

307. Choose your instructors carefully. Being an expert doesn't always translate into being an expert presenter or a caring teacher.

308. Use open-ended questions to *invite* conversation, and closed-ended (yes/no) questions to bring one to a close.

309. Don't let your charity come at the expense of someone's dignity.

To put it bluntly, nobody wants to feel like a charity case. Rather than imposing your goodwill on someone who might not be comfortable with it, ask, "Would you let me?"

You might hear, "No." Better to respect an honest no than to force a yes and taint the relationship.

The respect you show others, particularly in the low points of their lives, will be remembered long after your good deeds. Ironically, showing respect also makes it easier for your good deeds to be accepted.

310. Never cook bacon in the nude.

311. Expect a few hassles when you fly. Prepare for them.

312. Give yourself permission to cry.

Then again, if you're weeping over a Merrill Lynch ad, like Robert De Niro in *Analyze This*, you might want to get that checked out. (Sorry. Just trying to lighten the mood.)

All kidding aside, don't be ashamed of tears— they're a sign of our humanity, and sometimes they're absolutely necessary. Make friends with people who understand this, and who aren't going to dork out if you need to cry now and then.

313. Before you buy or rent your next home, make sure you'll be able to get a good pizza delivered.

314. Get to know an organization for at least two years before adding them to your will.

315. Don't let your kids whine.

> As my mother used to say, "I can't understand you unless you speak like an adult." It worked. We rarely whined.

316. Beware the person whose unspoken motto is, "The rules don't apply to me."

317. Wrap up your phone calls long before bedtime. You'll sleep better.

318. Take good care of your back.

319. When faced with two good options, choose the one you'll want to look back on a year from now.

320. Say no to political correctness and yes to good manners.

It's politically correct to call a Christmas tree a holiday tree. It's good manners to respect that not everyone celebrates Christmas.

321. Be big enough to step inside other people's worlds.

322. Beware the organization whose response to a burning building is to form a committee.

323. Carry yourself with a sense of urgency, and tune in to *other* people's urgency.

324. For a closer look at what urgency is and how it plays out within organizations, read John P. Kotter's book, *A Sense of Urgency*.

stuffyoualreadyknow.com/324

325.

When someone criticizes you unjustly, look the critic in the eye and say, "I don't accept that."

326. Money isn't the only thing that compounds— knowledge and skill do, too. The sooner you acquire these things, the longer you'll have to use and develop them.

327. Listen to "The Final Bell" off the *Rocky* soundtrack, and try telling me this world can keep you down. It can't.

328. Seek out stories of those who have overcome the hardest circumstances imaginable. The world is filled with these stories.

329. Know when to treat your kids equally, and when to treat them uniquely.

330. Look for a boss who doesn't hesitate to recognize and reward high performance.

331. Remember that no one ever lost friends for not sharing vacation photos.

332. When you know what you need to do, do it.

Sometimes we need to sit through a seminar on how to get organized—most times, we just need to go clean our office.

333. Set boundaries for yourself, not for other people.

One night when my nephew Dylan was about five, he and his older siblings got together with the other neighborhood kids for "night games." Dylan is the closest thing our family has to a minister. He's also a born athlete—so when the captains chose up teams and Dylan was picked last, he stormed off the field and shouted, *"I don't have to take this sh*t!"*

And he didn't. As adults, we don't willingly sign up for unacceptable treatment—but over time, it can creep in and start to appear normal. Some examples:

- The friend who's in constant crisis mode, and for whom no amount of your help will ever be enough.

- The co-worker who has forty-five minutes to drop by to tell you how busy he is.

- The client who misses deadlines and expects you to pick up the slack.

- The talented but hotheaded employee who wreaks havoc on office morale.

- Anyone who repeatedly breaks commitments to you, even minor ones.

You can't control these folks. But you *can* decide what you will and won't put up with. That, in a nutshell, is what it means to set a boundary.

334. Never apologize for having boundaries. Without them, you will suffer needlessly and cause suffering for those around you.

335. Eat a big breakfast. You'll feel better and eat more sensibly the rest of the day.

336. Make your commute time count.

If you use just two hours per week to listen to something inspiring or educational, that adds up to more than 100 hours, or 2.5 workweeks, over a year's time. What could you learn in a hundred hours?

stuffyoualreadyknow.com/336

337. Don't ask personal questions, especially about people who aren't in the room.

338. Choose your words carefully. You can apologize for harsh words, but you can never take them back.

339. Don't assume everyone shares your political or religious worldview.

340. Treat yourself to a shoe-shine when passing through an airport.

341. Avoid foolish arguments, including the ones inside your own head.

This is another place where deep breathing helps. I have learned it's impossible to breathe deeply and get drawn into an argument at the same time—or to breathe deeply and hold on to destructive thoughts.

When the conflict is on the outside, taking a few deep breaths makes the situation easier to diffuse—usually with very few words, or no words at all.

342.

Celebrate your accomplishments, especially the big ones.

You could do this with bling, such as a Montblanc pen. You could do it with an experience—maybe dinner at your favorite high-end restaurant. Or you could celebrate with an investment in yourself.

I know one woman who, after writing her first book, scheduled a weekend yoga retreat. That wouldn't be *my* thing, and it might not be yours. But you get the idea.

Choose something memorable and fun, and fitting for the accomplishment you're celebrating.

343. Don't be competitive about things that were never meant to be a competition.

344. Live so the saying, "What goes around comes around" is a promise, not a threat.

345. Beware the person whose need to be needed is greater than your need.

346. Postpone taking action when you're hungry, angry, lonely, or tired, otherwise known as HALT.

347. When all else fails, tell it like it is.

"You can't offend a car salesman."
—my mom, trying (privately) to get me to stop tiptoeing around while negotiating for my first car

348. Do not put anyone on a pedestal. If you do, you'll end up under one.

349. The person who wants less closeness in a relationship is the one who sets the pace. Respect that person's wishes, even when that person is you.

350. Generally speaking, let other people fight their own battles.

351. When giving a speech, give one speech, not three. Many an audience has tuned out because the speaker just couldn't land the plane.

stuffyoualreadyknow.com/351

352. Be careful not to overcrowd a room with furniture and knickknacks—that's the best way to make the room seem bigger.

stuff YOU already know…

353. Remember that people buy emotionally and justify rationally.

354. Say a short, silent prayer when you hear an ambulance.

355. When choosing carpet or paint colors, evaluate each one separately—and obviously in the room where you'll be putting them.

356. Read the editorial section of your favorite newspaper.

The Opinion section of *The Wall Street Journal* is one of my favorites—including and especially the letters to the editor. Reading others' well-formed opinions will give you a much broader and more interesting perspective on the news.

357. Don't confuse love with obsession.

358.

When things go wrong, always be willing to acknowledge your role.

That's how you grow and get unstuck.

359. Rule #1 in self-defense: "Don't be at the fight."

360. Before you go to bed at night, shine your kitchen sink. (Thank you, flylady.net, for that surprisingly great tip.)

361. Remember that the best revenge isn't living well. The best revenge is being good: good at heart, good at what you do, good to everyone you meet.

362. Don't start a sentence with, "I'll be honest …" Just be honest, and trust others to see it.

363. Read *The 7 Habits of Highly Effective People* by Stephen R. Covey.

stuffyoualreadyknow.com/363

364. Appreciate new places for what they are. Resist the temptation to compare them with home.

365. Use coupons only for things you would have bought anyway. If you're spending fifty dollars to save ten, you're still out forty dollars.

366. Not everything needs to be talked about. Not everything needs to be responded to. Save your energy for the things that do.

367. Don't assume someone doesn't love you just because they don't show it in the way you would like.

368. Treat younger adult siblings like adults, not the way you remember them when they were twelve.

stuff YOU already know...

369. Don't try to be like people half your age. Live so they want to be like you.

370. Live so each one of your grandchildren thinks he or she is the favorite.

371. Even if you live to be ninety, try not to use the word "ointment."

372. Don't let children interrupt. But when it *is* their turn to speak, listen to them with your full attention.

373. Do something at least twice a year for kids in foster care.

374. Try not to call someone's hometown airport *cute*, even if it is. It's like calling a grown man *adorable*. (I did that once. It did not go over well.)

375. Even if you live in Seattle, wear sunscreen daily—especially on your face.

The key is to find one you like, so you *will* use it daily. Ever notice how many sunscreens burn your eyes or go on like clown white? My friend Ann found one that does neither: EltaMD UV Physical Broad-Spectrum SPF 41, available from a dermatologist or on Amazon.

stuffyoualreadyknow.com/375

stuff YOU already know…

376.

Honor your limitations.

377. Let yourself move on.

When my nephew James had just turned two, his dad took him trick-or-treating for the first time. Each time they went to a house, knocked on the door, and received candy, James would want to sort of camp out there. He didn't get the concept of one per customer.

More importantly, he was too young to appreciate that there was *more* candy—maybe even better candy—waiting for him down the street.

So it is sometimes with us. We camp out in one place too long—a job, a membership, a relationship—hoping in vain for the equivalent of one more Snickers bar.

Life often has better things in store for us, if only we can tear ourselves away and walk a little farther down the street.

378. Let other people move on.

379.

Don't remind people of their less-than-perfect past.

In the words of Oscar Wilde, "Every saint has a past, and every sinner has a future."

380. In addition to being a good driver, be a good pedestrian.

> Yes, as a pedestrian you have the right-of-way—but the guy in the Chrysler has your life in his hands.

381. Offer to walk a woman to her car, especially after dark.

382. Speak in terms of the other person's time zone.

383. Beware the so-called spiritual person who has no sense of humor.

384. Beware the pastor who's got nothing *but* humor.

385. Develop an appreciation for food and music, and you'll be able to talk to just about anyone, anywhere.

Special thanks to my former boss, who gave me permission to share this story. The two of us had a good laugh about the fact that he barely remembers it.

One day my boss returned to the office, only to find his staff had shamelessly and unanimously shot down his instructions to plan an office social.

Granted, overthrowing his idea was immature on our part. On the other hand, we just weren't feeling it. Besides, nothing bonds a disjointed team like a bit of good-old-fashioned mutiny. Nixing the office get-together did more to unite us than any other group activity—so in that sense, mission accomplished, right?

Our boss saw it differently. In a rare display of anger, he required each of us to give a written account of how we spent the Tuesday afternoon that had been set aside for fun and team-building. Here's what I wrote:

I went to see the internship supervisor at the Community Media Center. Was greeted by a tall guy with dreadlocks. I asked him, "What smells so good?" I figured it was the Rib Crib, the restaurant across the street. He told me it's his chicken fricassee, he made it himself, and he's willing to share recipes. We shake hands and introduce ourselves. His name is Steve.

So after I'm done with my meeting (which went very well), Steve calls me into his office, sits me down, and serves me a warm bowl of rice and beans, with his chicken fricassee on top. Damn, it was good! A little spicy, but who cares? He had also written out the recipe for me. So I'm now the proud owner of a recipe for Jamaican Chicken Fricassee.

We sat and talked about food and music, and how those two topics allowed you to talk to just about anyone, anywhere. We traded business cards. I owe him a recipe for Aunt Anne's meatballs. He said

stuff YOU already know…

he would follow up with the rice and beans recipe.
Secret ingredient: coconut milk!

Shaking hands, breaking bread, and moving
the office mission forward: That's *real* fun—not
playing croquet, which had been one of the
suggestions for the office social.

A few months after the group rebellion, our
office agreed to get together and paint bowls
for a local soup kitchen. This time, the mission
truly *was* accomplished. In all of my career, it
was one of the most memorable and rewarding
office bonding experiences I can remember. No
awkward exercises, no Kumbaya, just a group of
people getting together and getting creative for
a cause outside ourselves.

stuffyoualreadyknow.com/385

386.

Never compromise your safety.

stuff YOU already know…

387. Don't let anyone steal your good mood
or good spirits.

388. Don't let anyone steal your dreams.

389. Learn how to gracefully take hints.

390. Respect other people's desire to be left alone at
the gym. And on airplanes.

391. Don't get serious with anyone who's
been in your life less time than the
box of baking soda.

Especially since ARM & HAMMER started
recommending we change the box every thirty
days instead of every ninety days.

392. Don't waste time on music or art that "should" appeal to you, but doesn't.

393. Be assertive, but don't be aggressive. Notice how often aggression covers up a *lack* of assertiveness.

394. Before you exceed expectations, meet them.

395. When the spirit moves you, reach out to a long-lost friend.

Steve Dumas was a larger-than-life character who lived across the street from us when I was a kid. He was a couple of years older than my oldest brother, and it was always sort of a thrill whenever he came over.

In addition to being a football star and the friendliest kid in town, he had this Alabama twang that made him exotic to us Midwestern kids.

stuff YOU already know…

Steve and his family moved back to Alabama when I was in second grade, never to be heard from again. Before he left, we acquired his dog: a beagle named Sadie. Best dog ever.

Last summer, I was sharing the story of Sadie with my nephew Dylan—and about a month later, my mom came across Steve Dumas on LinkedIn.

Keep in mind, we hadn't heard from him since the *Nixon* era. Can you imagine? He was still living in Alabama, working in his family's furniture business, married with four beautiful kids.

Steve and the DeLapas have since traded a handful of emails, reminiscing about the Coloma (Michigan) days and catching up on one another's lives.

This is probably the closest I'll ever come to seeing someone raised from the dead.

Steve and I don't write often, but when we do,

we never stop marveling at how amazing it is to be in touch.

Last December, I sent him a picture of my Christmas tree—the first one I had put up or felt compelled to put up in probably fifteen years. It was the happiest tree I had ever seen, mirroring one of the happiest times in my life.

Within minutes of hitting Send, my phone was buzzing. It was Steve Dumas, with words that sparkled like strings of lights. He ended by wishing my loved ones and me a blessed Christmas, and his note was signed, "Your Friend Forever, Steve."

The one thing missing from my Christmas tree had been a crowning star. After reading Steve's note, I looked up and could almost see one—beaming from here to Alabama and back.

396. When your mind is made up, avoid lengthy explanations.

397. Don't expect another person to make you happy—that's *your* job.

398. Keep your kitchen knives sharp. Dull knives are more dangerous than sharp ones.

399. Before starting a new recipe, read it all the way through so you're not caught off guard.

stuffyoualreadyknow.com/399

400. Growth doesn't always tickle. Grow anyway.

As my mother often told me as I was growing up, "If you're going to grow, you're going to have to leave some people behind." What I realized later is that sometimes the person we need to leave behind is the old us.

401. Remember that the government that is big enough to give you everything you want is big enough to take away everything you have.

402. Be driven not by a fear of dying but by a passion for living.

403. Work hard, but don't become a workaholic. You need a life outside of work.

404. When necessary and appropriate, ask the hard questions. Chances are, other people are wanting to know the same thing.

405. Preserve your mental health at all costs.

406. Brush your teeth after lunch.

stuff YOU already know…

407. Commit yourself to writing well. We write only as clearly as we think.

408. Resist the temptation to pull up the flowers to see how they're doing.

409. Don't chat up a woman on an elevator.

410. Network only with those you like, trust, and respect.

411. Put your energy into the present and the future, not the past.

412. Before you vacation with friends, make sure you're looking for the same kind of vacation.

413.

Beware the insult dipped in sugar.

This generally includes anything that starts with, "Bless your heart."

414. Don't rehash to death things that are already settled. Move forward.

415. Know when to repeat a good memory, and when simply to relive it.

stuffyoualreadyknow.com/415

416. If you ever get a storage unit, make sure it's on the first level, even if it costs a bit more. You'll be glad not to have to mess with an elevator.

417. Don't phone or text during the dinner hour.

418. Don't put people on the spot.

For example, when you were in the womb, Adam, your mother kept getting the question, "Are you hoping for a boy or a girl?" She would always want to say, "We've really got our hearts set on a boy, and it (blankety-blank) well better not be anything different."

---

419. Don't ask couples when they're going to have kids—or when they're going to stop.

420. Love those in your care with fierceness and gusto. As my dad once told me, "I'd kick a dragon's ass for you."

421. Before you preach, listen. Everybody's got a story. By the time you hear it, you might forget all about what you were going to say.

422. Don't underestimate the power of a good affirmation.

Every morning during an extended stay with my parents, I would write in my journal, "I am a good and gracious guest."

Granted, my parents and I always enjoy our visits. But this one was like one big Norman Rockwell painting. I think it was the affirmations.

When I shared this story with my friend Ginna, she wrote back with a few affirmations of her own:

- I am a good and gracious guest.
- I will not call the airline to move up my departure.
- I do not want to slap my brother in the mouth.
- She didn't mean that I looked fat.
- Despite having explained the truth numerous times, I will go along with the story that I am responsible for the house fire of '73.
- I will not dump the plate of spaghetti on any relative.

Affirmations might be corny, but they work. The silly ones get us to laugh, and the serious ones keep us on the right track. Experts say the best affirmations are positive, present tense, and personal.

423. Learn how to take constructive feedback. Even when it's poorly delivered, take whatever truth and value it contains, and let the rest go.

424. Easy way to class up a spinach salad: Tear off the stems before adding the dressing. The whole thing will look better and taste better.

425. Don't settle for goals that don't excite you. What you want with all your heart, you'll go after with all your heart.

426. Make it a point not to complain when you're an out-of-town guest. Your host can't control the traffic or the weather.

427. Have a favorite restaurant to take out-of-town guests.

428. Have a favorite hotel where you can refer out-of-town guests.

429. Have houseguests only if you can do so cheerfully—and only for as long as you can do so cheerfully. When in doubt, err on the side of brevity.

430. Kid around only with those you like and who you know can take it well.

431. Get the thing you really want, even if it means delaying the purchase.

432. When your food craving isn't going away, indulge it. Otherwise, you'll probably end up eating twice.

433. Don't enter a hot dog eating contest.

434. If you work with people long enough, you're going to start having dreams about them. The mistake people make is in sharing those dreams.

435. Take comfort from my mother's words, "We may not have it all together—but together, we have it all."

436. Take courage from my father's words, "Together, we're stronger than *garlic*."

stuff YOU already know…

437.

Promise yourself you'll never give up.

Afterword

Remember that scene from *Walk the Line*, where Sam Phillips gives a young Johnny Cash his famous, "If you was hit by a truck" speech?

This book is my response—the best I have to offer. It says the things I would most want you to know, if I had only one chance to tell you. And if I haven't already said it somewhere in these pages, I'll say it now: I believe your life matters, infinitely.

As I wrap this up, there's a man outside my eighth-floor office, washing my windows. Never mind that the ropes on which his life depends are about as big around as my thumbs. My world is brighter for his having been here.

So may it be for you, with this book. May your world be brighter for having read it, and may it inspire you to go set your world on fire—not literally, and not someday, but starting right this moment.

stuffyoualreadyknow.com/thankyou

Acknowledgments

My heartfelt gratitude to all the friends and family members who lent me their wisdom, prayers, stories, and high fives. I especially wish to thank the following people:

Gail Gersonde, for her friendship and for making me Aunt Gina to her son Adam. Lake Michigan Catholic Middle School made us friends—God made us "fambly."

My parents, **Jim and Judy DeLapa,** whose love, wisdom, reverence, and irreverence are evident on every page. Thank you forever for all your love and support.

My nephews and nieces **Justin, Sarah, Dylan, James, Maureen, and Michelle**—the lifeblood of our family and the joy of my heart.

Seth Kahan of visionaryleadership.com, who sensed my initial excitement for this project, and actively encouraged me to follow where it led.

Jeniffer Thompson, Aleta Reese, Julio Pompa Frizza and the entire team at Monkey C Media, for designing a book jacket and interior that surpassed my wildest dreams—and for graciously going the extra mile to make it happen.

An extra shout-out to **Jeniffer Thompson,** who from our first phone call caught the vision of this project, shared my enthusiasm, and shared her contacts—a threefold act of generosity that rocked my world and rocked this book.

Mary Altbaum, my copyeditor and proofreader, for her insight, encouragement, flexibility, and editorial fine-tooth comb. I am a better editor for having worked with you.

Jared Kuritz and Antoinette Kuritz of STRATEGIES Public Relations, whose energy and vision for this project added immeasurably to my own. Thank you for expanding my world and exceeding all expectations.

God, the Author of Life, who grew my excitement for this project, the more I turned it over to Him. May all of this be Your work more than mine.